Dedication

I would like to dedicate this book to several people. Firstly, my mother for staying on my back and being vigilant about a young boy making a promise to take care of his mom through his scribbling on paper. Secondly, to all the women who inspired me to creatively use the alphabet to express my emotions and give life to our story. Thirdly, to my partner in creativity who pushes me to bear my soul because that's where the good stuff is. Lastly, all the poets whom I've had the pleasure of meeting over the years and most importantly the Cleveland poetry community, for nurturing me as a writer and encouraging me as a performer. So I just want to say God bless you all for being a big part of my life.

Unbridled Love

Her smile illuminates the darkness of the room
It warms my insides
Allowing me to stand exposed in a January snow fall
It would quench my thirst in the hottest of desserts
What manner of love is this?
Uninhibited
Unbridled
Unforced
Natural
Raw
Excepting all flaws
Small square and all

The M.C. & The D.J.

I see myself
Living inside your pretty brown eyes
I found a home between your thighs
Then realized
Our hearts beat on the same time line
Music be our lifeline
Sex
Is how we pass time
Writing on paper is where we find
The intersection of our connection
Lying on the fault line of Love and heartache
We find reality where the beat breaks
That is why we're each other's perfect date

Stolen Secrets

I was clay in your hands
Asking to be molded into your
Mr. Right
With a Mister Goodnight vibe
You know from the Zulu Mandingo tribe
Because I love trimming the bush
Slapping the tush
And it might get a little freaky
If I open mouth an insert foot

I Love the sounds you made as your body shook
I was hooked
Before you called me daddy
Remnants of me on your sheets
And your scent
Inside stolen wet panties
If you want them back, call me!

The Honeymoon

White sand beaches
Palm trees
Mexico sea breezes
Sombreros & bikinis
Blue water & beautiful sunsets
Let's go half on baby

The mood is set
No rain but your wet
I need you at 6:30
Me at 3
We fit together perfectly
It had to be destiny

I filled your womb with my seed
Believe me
We are a true trinity
Following the path and rules of divinity
Jesus pieces are plenty
Like sinfully given Christianity

But our halos have been spit shined an
Merged like twine
As we toast our love
We've transformed water into wine
The two becomes one at this time

Softest lips

You've got the softest lips that God has ever made
Don't be embarrassed or ashamed
I'll kiss both sets and the intensity will be the same
I want to make you squirt for days
So when I dive in
I'll make waves

Add a little whip cream and chocolate
And you could be my personal Sundae
Or maybe you like chains and whips
Nipple clamps and hot candle wax

Or you're a head doctor
Come an examine me
And if you swallow,
Well u can definitely be
My P.C.P

Simple Lover

She was my Dark chocolate angel with bangles
With a smile so heavenly
Her attitude ghetto and at the ready
Body firm like an old school Chevy
She didn't know it but at hello
She was mine already

My conversation was witty
My hand on her inner thigh
Hmmmmm sticky
Hopped on the 3 Superior
East to westbound
SWV, going downtown
Made her legs flutter like butterfly wings
Not a head doctor
But a cunnilinguist king

She called me Daddy between breaths
Protected me like chess
Her Becky
Is the fucking best
I screamed her name before she was done
I knew she was the one
Head game was bucket
The sex was
And 1

Secret Fantasies

I had a vision of you on your tippy toes
Lace windows let the twins be exposed
Supple suckles on nipples as the tongue rolls
Leaving traces of moisture on soft skin
We turnin' up the heat in the kitchen
The blinds are open
Our actions in full view
So I carried you to the island to taste you
I dive in head first
It gets wet and soupy
No hands, no utensils
Your moans made our soundtrack instrumental
When u came no juices were wasted
My face.....Well basted
Was that Pineapples I Tasted?

See your so beautiful naked
Now I know what Adam must have been faced wit
But I see the table is vacant
And I always wanted to Butter yo roll on it
I love the sounds you make while I'm hitting it.
But calling me daddy is a little more than I can deal wit
I just hate that it was all dream
What a trip

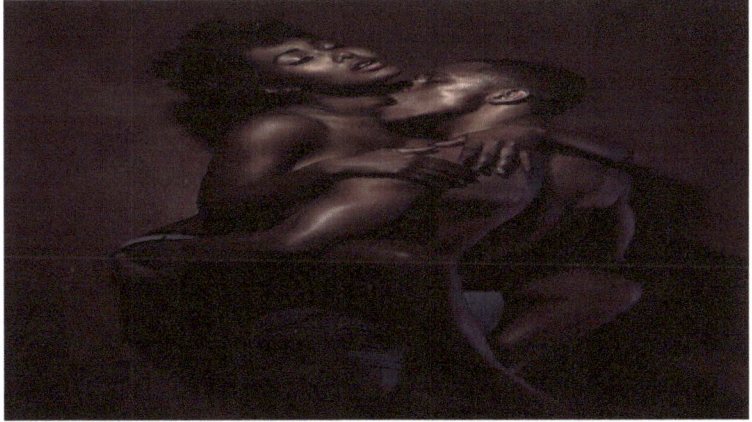

S.C.U.B.A.

My Tongue parts lips for deep penetration
The ultimate stimulation
Searching the whole cavity
Deep enough to tickle your tonsils
Weaken your knees
Turn frowns upside down
Deliver sounds of pleasure

Three days it took me to find your treasure
On the raft or wherever
Waves will be made
Heart rates will be raised
Apologies may be given after the orgasm parade
Tucked her in
She's done for the day
Call me Sinatra
I did it my way

QUIET STORM

Overcast skies are a sign that a storm is brewing

Possibility of moisture is on the rise

Inside the sun is shining brightly on thoughts of fantasy

and escapades

She wants an upgrade

Have her precipitation turn into a torrential downpour

She's no whore, but today she wants her insides

explored

She wants to make her king roar

She's decided there's no need for the bed

She wants to feel the cold of the floor

The stiffness of the wood

Making her walls crumble is just not good enough

She wants her wildest dreams to come true

And this morning she will be the storm that cums

Protector

I'm looking in your eyes for shelter
And you closed the blinds
As if I committed a crime
I was hoping you would be my warmth from the elements
My shepherd out of this storm
I fell believing you would catch me
Guess I was wrong
An anomaly
In limbo
Writing you love notes
Between humming bird wing stokes
Love you more than most would
More than I should
Death is not always easy
But sometimes
Only sometimes
It's good.

Perfect Rx

I love being in your presence
Breathing in your essence
When I'm with you I feel like a king
Instead of a peasant
In your arms my soul feels effervescent
Though my heart is hesitant
I'm safe in this place
Displaced anger being erased
But my emotions are Written All Over My Face
No Rude Boy
Romantic helplessly
If I touched you
Then you've felt me
Side effects (euphoria, orgasms, and drowsiness)
Perfect Rx -

Penned

I'm longing to be her poem
Write my most sensual lines
On her inner thigh
Craft orgasms out of haikus

This is not easy
Perfectly placed kisses
Sound cheesy
But an icy tongue tip
On hot lips
Makes her insides tense

If you want to have your insides autographed
Call me
Satisfaction guaranteed
I got references believe

Morning Dew

The sound of her morning shower routine
Brings a smile to my face
The image of water
Rolling down the nape of her neck
Has me feeling vexed
In the bathroom
I see her silhouette
I grow erect
I enter the shower to get wet
Kissing the 3rd&4th vertebrae of her neck
My hands hug her curves like corvettes
She bends over to deliver her pitch
The soap drops
I hit her spot from the back nonstop
Until I heard the door knocks
Our neighbors must have called the cops
They said that "they got reports of a possible murder happening"
I replied" No sir"
Just screams of pleasure and a little flesh slappin
Fuck makin the bed rock
We made the shower shake
And I bet the neighbors know my name

Missed

I miss you like days without responsibility
The security in your arms when you hold me
The light from your smile
I was yours at hello

I remember the first time seeing the moon cry
with your eyes
We lay together
No words
Our bodies spoke to each other in palpations
Our eyes connected our hearts like WI-FI
I still remember the hair on my neck standing up
during our first kiss
Truth is
I just miss U…

Michael Jackson Tribute

I wanna be Startin Sumthin with you

Let my Human Nature

Give you Butterflies

Because you're a PYT

A Thriller to me

A Dirty Diana possibly

Billy Jean maybe

BAD definitely

I wanna Beat It till you SCREAM

We cream

I Love The Way U Make Me Feel

Emotions bouncing Off The Wall

You Rock My World and

I just can't stop Loving U

So let's Remember The Time

Because The Girl is Mine

All mine!!!

LOVE STRINGS

I saw you thru tempered glass and
Fell in love with you
As soon as our eyes met
I had to have you

I desired to caress your neck gently
Hold your body close to mine
Exchange vibrations as
My fingertips manipulated the cords of your spine
Enjoying an intimacy that only sound can explain.

I love your attire
The way it drapes across your frame
Glossy, wood grain, asymmetrical
Custom designed
Accessories minimal
Our connection is nothing less than spiritual
You were made for me

Your voice
Heavenly
When warmed up and fine tuned
It's majestic
It can calm the savage beast
or bring tears to the gods
you put up no facades
Genuine like air

You seem so comfortable tucked inside your custom made covers
I was made to be your lover
Strum strings to cords
That make my blood boil
My heart race
This must be fate
I've been yours since eight sideways
But as I gaze at you in the arms of another,
I realize I don't know how to play the guitar.

Love Jones

I wanna be your Love Jones
Place soft kisses on your inner thigh
Be the reason you moan when home alone
On your essence
I wanna get gone
Bring you to tears of joy as we climax together

I plan to deliver tsunami-gasms
Multiple positions & ass slapping
Throw in a few toys wit' some oral action
See we ain't making love
This is a coronation of passion
The scene has been set
Can we make that happen?

Holiday Cheer

Tis' the season of miracles & bless…sins
So let's start by undress…sin'
Slowly caress…sin flesh
Lips to your breast and
My one wish for Christmas
Is to wrap you in mistletoe & kiss underneath where it sits
Get you wet & see if my Yule log fits
I want to be the only Jolly fat guy bringing you gifts tonight
So if you'll be my Ho Ho Ho
There will be no silent night…

High School Lovers

My High school sweetheart
I loved her dearly
She'd wear my jersey on game days, Really!
See, I'm in the mood for love whenever she's near me
She's got me up in the air like a wheelie
Can we go steady?
Pick one
Yes, no, or maybe
Freddie said it best
You are my lady
My… popcorn love
My… under the bleacher kisses
My… let me just put the head in wishes
My… two straws and one shake dream date
My… where you think you gon put that thing…
scream fate
My… prom queen
My... mean mug
My…graduation day first hug
My… first crush
My… first shared seat on the bus
My… first US

Hard Working

Her voice excites me
It gets my heartbeat up like P.T.
We match up perfectly like E harmony
Or maybe

I'm a Prince
You know charming
Game so tight they call it virgin
If you're the highway
I'm thinking bout merging

Wielding my hammer like Thor
While you scream for more
When it's over we heavy breathin'
You glowin'
Dimple showin'
Breakfast in bed the next mornin'
Alarm rings
I'm growin'
Kisses on your should blade has you moanin'
If sexin' you is a sin
I want to commit it with you once again

Good Morning

Woke up this morning feeling freaky
Look down and seen a Tepee
Rolled over to kissed her neck gently
Her eyes opened to see hard wood
Laid it on soft lips and pealed back the hood
She ask, "Can I"
My reply
"I wish you would"
Purple body kisses feel so good
It was a helleva morning in Mr. Johnson's neighborhood.....

Deeper than Lust

Today I want to maximize pressure in short strokes
Turn yo legs into goal posts
I want to be in so deep
That I can hear the air you gulp
Between long strokes
I'm in no mood to be tender wit' it
My goal
Is to have yo walls wailing in less than 20 min
Relieve all yo stress and
Make yo Juice Box wet
Have yo thighs shaking like a bottle of Moét
So when she popped
We be Mo' wet
18mins for the whole set
The look on yo face... Priceless
She looked at me like she was in a trance
Like I had her lost in space
Screaming till the next episode
Danger Danger....
You're in control.

Cruising

When I look into your eyes
I see the sunrises of our futures
You're the Coretta to my Martin Luther
And my dream is to crown you my Queen

I watch you sleep to understand life's meaning
Because the way you breathe is soothing
The rhythm of your heartbeat is moving
Being in love with you is like cruising
Top down
Stars out
Mouth on mouth
Hands flow down south
It's no doubt
69 should definitely be
A new in-her state route

Complete Ecstasy

She
kissed
me
with a passion that's been held captive for years.
I could taste her scent.
I let my tongue get caught in the creases of her mouth
as I traced her lips,
Finishing with a trail of soft "may I continue" contacts
down her cheek.
I tasted her chin

She
touches
me
with an ecstasy of young love.
We hold hands like old love.
I hold her like forgotten love.
But remember the sweep of her hand across my face,
Mine around her waist.
It's peaceful here.
In the void between rain and rainbows

I
Licked
her
with devotion as if she, was a deity.
Like her skin was candy coated.
From the space behind her ear lobe
to the back of her neck, just below her hair line
Then, I made a bee line down her spine
Just below bikini lines
Alphabet tricks
These ain't for kids
But was amazed, when I realized,
That she licked me 34,
I licked her 35 times
In different directions
Confession
I liked it

Continued.

I
stroked
her
with a zest of new love
I experienced all of her
Hands tangled in her hair like a tight grip
her moans cascaded off the walls like faint laughter as I try to free myself
I give her all of me
Deeply
I feel her insides collapse around me
As her hips move with a conviction that this obelisk is hers
Our essence collided with the ferocity of a train crash
Sending both our bodies into an apoplexy like movement
Our heartbeats chase each other to a normal pace

We
Nibbled
Each other
with teeth tickling nerve endings that have already been frazzled.
Creating aftershocks of sensations seemingly unbearable we offer up no resistance.
We lay together regretless
Gazing into each other's eyes.
Trying to see the insecurities in our souls
I speak with confidence
she waits
I'm rejuvenated
You ready.

Collegiate Love story pt 1

She was my Sensei
My Mrs. Mi-ah-gi
She taught me how to satisfy a woman's body
And I was the perfect student
Listened intently
Sacrificed my time willingly
Practiced diligently
She brought out the best in me literally

Now I know foreplay starts from that last encounter
You build it up till it's like gun powder
Then you rub & caress it
Pet & prime it
Perforate it until it leaks
Mission not complete
Until you put the wick in it
Light it & let it blow

Sooo
I learned to start slow
Vary my tempo & positions
And incorporate other erogenous zones
I started given big O's in multiples
Mute girls became audible
The word got out and this fat guy became adorable
Due to some dexterous oral & javelin skills
I earned my black belt in erotica
Now I'm a bedroom monstah
It ain't Face book but
If you sign on I will poke ya......

Collegiate Love story pt 2

I had to choose between two
North vs. South
Light skin long hair
The big apple won out
Shorty had a fly mouth
Venus no doubt
I really liked her
Loved, was more like it
Paraded me around the Airmen campus
Caressed each other for one night
Life was made
I stayed
She faded away
First son returned to God
Bad news lands hard on drunken ears
But I still cried sober tears
I missed that connection for 20 yrs
Then Face book brought 500 miles within keystrokes & a poke
Now with plans to never be separated
Friendship reconnected from '88
Damn Face book is like Tony the tiger
Ggggggreat....

Cavernous Love

Let me pour into you
Replenish your reservoir with my kisses
Invigorate you cerebrally with torrential downpours of passion
Falling ever so lightly on the most delicate parts of your skin

I can taste the cravings that I have for you
Developing in the posterior of my throat
And there essence is flavorful

So I consume it slowly, relishing its value
Before ravishing the frame of a goddess worthy of these carnal thoughts
Nothing I want to do to you is simple
Just disclose to me the hour to which we shall sojourn...

Beautiful Wish

I wished for lavender kisses that reeked of passion
Silk touches that map quest my most sensual zones
I want to hear your most pleasurable moans
Please, don't hold back we grown
And when I look into your eyes
I want to feel the security of home

Baby I gave u a ring tone
You're my Love Jones
We got that unbridled love
Like midnight back rubs
Rose petal covered conversations in bath tubs and
Moans that become applauses of gratification
And I bow in acceptance of your release
During orgasms breathing may cease
Covering me with your essence
I hold u after for peace.

 It's beautiful to watch you sleep
In the calm of aligned heartbeats
On 1000 Count bed sheets
Even in the space between life & death
Your smile still radiates beautifully

You make me feel like the first snowfall at the end of summer
Like the moon smiling, when the Sun goes down
Like breathing
Believe me I crave you
I just hope you wish for me as well.

A...Muse

I want you to be my perfect poem
Let us cum together to create the perfect harmony
Duets cum naturally
As you suck my soul
I will lick your funky emotions
Then fuck you human
As you swallow my essence
Our Bond tightens
Closeness is accepted
Man down
Code 10
Oh wait....RESSURECTED!

3 D

From across the room
Eye contact was made
My head turns to watch her hips sway

In that glimpse frozen in time
Your fears became mine
I saw the caterpillar in your eyes
Ready to release your inner butterfly

With no regrets
My confession is…
I want more than hot sex

I want to be your backbone
You can consider me home
Past sins against you
I want to atone for

Think beyond the sun…
Shine on me
You're my Ms. Heavenly…

Body of a goddess
I'm a witness
In you I see God's artistry
Monet maybe…

Picasso possibly
Melting together like Salvador Dali
Could we be the Adam & Eve of a new beginning

Like the 3D's
Devotion, dedication and divinity
We are all encompassing